DUE DATE	BRODART	03/97	21.50

Our Endangered Planet
ANTARCTICA

Suzanne Winckler

and

Mary M. Rodgers

with a foreword by Will Steger

LERNER PUBLICATIONS COMPANY • MINNEAPOLIS

Thanks to Dr. Donald Siniff, James E. Laib, Bill Kauffmann, Zach Marell, and Gary Hansen for their help in preparing this book.

Words in **bold** type are listed in a glossary that starts on page 59.

LIBRARY OF CONGRESS CATALOGING-IN-PUBLICATION DATA

Winckler, Suzanne, 1946-
    Our endangered planet. Antarctica / Suzanne Winckler and Mary M. Rodgers.
        p.   cm.
    Includes bibliographical references and index.
    Summary: An introduction to the world's coldest continent, its explorations, its wildlife, and its role in the global environment.
    ISBN 0-8225-2506-2 (lib. bdg.)
    1. Antarctic regions—Juvenile literature. [1. Anatarctic regions.]
I. Rodgers, Mary M. (Mary Madeline), 1954-   . II. Title.
G863.W56
919.8'9—dc20   91-22899
                                                         CIP
                                                          AC

Manufactured in the United States of America
    2 3 4 5 6 7 8 9 10 01 00 99 98 97 96 95 94 93

Front cover: *Wearing protective clothing, a scientist in Antarctica waits for a group of king penguins to pass.*
Back cover: *(Left) A pair of southern elephant seals roar at each other during breeding season. (Right) Drums full of waste from research bases lie within sight of a docked tourist ship.*

Recycled paper

All paper used in this book is of recycled material and may be recycled.

Recyclable

CONTENTS

Will Steger led the International Trans-Antarctica Expedition that was the first to cross the continent by dogsled.

FOREWORD

Since I can remember, I have had a strong curiosity about the world. When I was 15, I took a boat down the Mississippi River from Minneapolis to New Orleans. Later, I traveled across unmapped areas of North America, visiting regions that were untouched by the modern world. On these trips, I saw no presence of modern people or of damage to nature.

But in recent years our demand for world resources has skyrocketed, damaging many untouched areas. My great concern about these harmful changes led me to write and lecture about the global environment. This concern became the driving force behind the 1990 International Trans-Antarctica Expedition.

In 1989, our team—representing six different nations and cultures—began to cross Antarctica by dogsled. It was a long, hard, exciting, treacherous journey. Our success demonstrated the power of international cooperation and the strength of the human spirit. When we reached the end of our expedition in March 1990, we had achieved two goals. First, we had finished what we had set out to do—we had crossed Antarctica. Second, our trek had focused the world's attention on the little-known, icy continent at the bottom of our planet.

Global attention is important right now, as world leaders are deciding Antarctica's future. It is my hope that all nations will join together to safeguard this polar region so it may serve as a shining example of international cooperation.

The more we know and understand our earth, the better prepared we are to protect and preserve its precious resources. That's why *Antarctica* is an important book. It teaches us about the continent's environment, unusual wildlife, and unique history. The book also helps us to understand the risk we take in dismissing Antarctica and its surrounding ocean as too far away to matter. In the end, everything on our planet matters.

WILL STEGER

5

OUR ENDANGERED PLANET

In the 1960s, astronauts first traveled beyond the earth's protective atmosphere and were able to look back at our planet. What they saw was a beautiful globe, turning slowly in space. That image reminds us that our home planet has limits, for we know of no other place that can support life.

The various parts of our natural environment—including air, water, soil, plants, and animals—are partners in making our planet a good place to live. If we endanger one element, the other partners are badly affected, too.

People throughout the world are working to protect and heal the earth's environment. They recognize that making nature our ally and not our victim is the way to shape a common future. Because we have only one planet to share, its health and survival mean that we all can live.

Humans have settled nearly all parts of our planet. We have changed the layout of the land by clearing trees to create farmland and cities. We have dammed rivers to produce energy and have dug into the ground to take out minerals. Yet the earth still has one place—the continent of Antarctica—where the effect of human actions has been slight.

Some people think that Antarctica contains valuable minerals that could be mined. Other people regard Antarctica as the earth's last wilderness, which should be preserved without change. For 30 years, an international treaty has protected Antarctica. Because the continent does not belong to any country, all of us have a role in preserving it. By learning as much as we can about this faraway place, we have a better chance of influencing the leaders who will decide Antarctica's future.

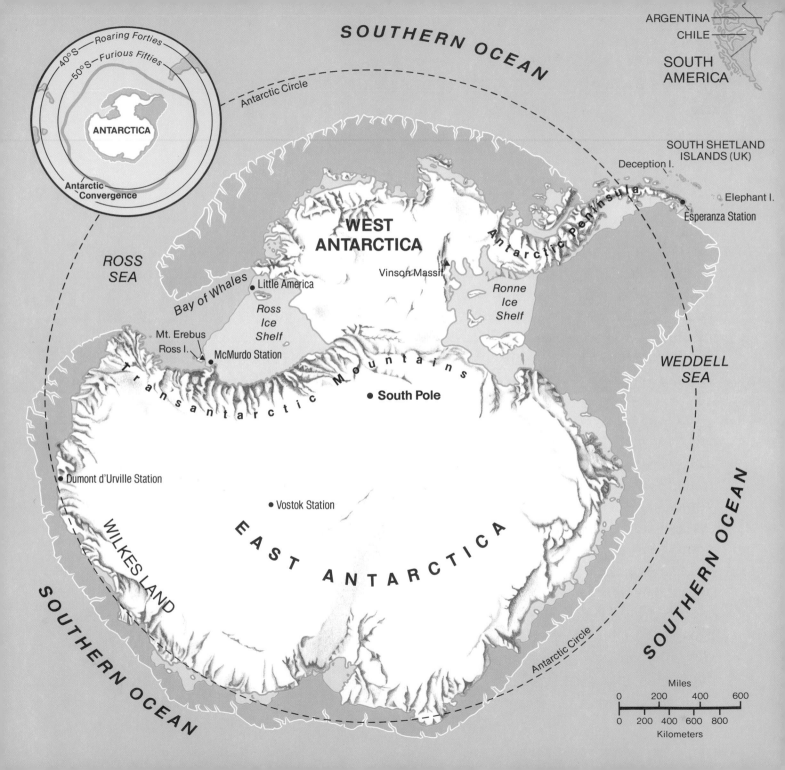

CHAPTER ONE

A PLACE OF EXTREMES

We humans cannot stand the cold very well. If you held an ice cube to your cheek, your skin would soon start to burn. Imagine an ice cube as big as the United States and Mexico combined. It exists! It is called Antarctica.

LIFE AT THE BOTTOM

The continent of Antarctica covers 5.4 million square miles (14 million square kilometers) of land. In winter, when the sea around Antarctica freezes, the continent looks like it has doubled in size.

To find Antarctica on a globe, you would have to turn the globe upside down. The continent surrounds the bottom of our planet—the South Pole. The water encircling Antarctica is the Southern Ocean. Some people prefer to say that the conti-

nent has shores on three oceans—the Pacific, the Indian, and the Atlantic.

Roughly shaped like a full-skirted dress, Antarctica has two large dents. The Ross Sea cuts into the waist of the dress from one side, and the Weddell Sea makes a notch in the other side.

The continent also has several regions. At one end is West (or Lesser) Antarctica, from which a narrow strip of land, the Antarctic Peninsula, extends like a sleeve. East (or Greater) Antarctica spans the full skirt. The Transantarctic Mountains cut between East and West Antarctica.

FIRE AND ICE

Between 50 million and 100 million years ago, powerful underground forces ripped off a large piece of South America. The torn piece of land, which took millions of years to move to its present place, is Antarctica. Still the closest continent to Antarctica, South America lies about 500 miles (805 kilometers) away.

When the earth's surface layer is torn, hot gases and a liquid rock called **magma** spew up from the deep center of our planet. Volcanoes form where this hot ma-

Sunlight shines on the ice surrounding Mount Erebus, an active volcano on Ross Island.

A cave that scientists cut into Antarctica's covering reveals the thickness of the continent's ice sheets.

terial breaks the ocean's surface. Two of the islands that encircle Antarctica—Ross Island and Deception Island—still have active volcanoes.

THE ICE THAT BINDS

Ice covers 98 percent of Antarctica. Without ice, Antarctica would consist of one

Because the snow in Antarctica rarely melts, it builds up over time into huge, dense masses of six-sided ice crystals. These drawings show (top) how pressure from the upper layers of ice makes the crystals line up. The pull of the earth's gravity and the weight of the ice then cause the mass of crystals to slide (bottom). The slowly moving ice mass is called a glacier.

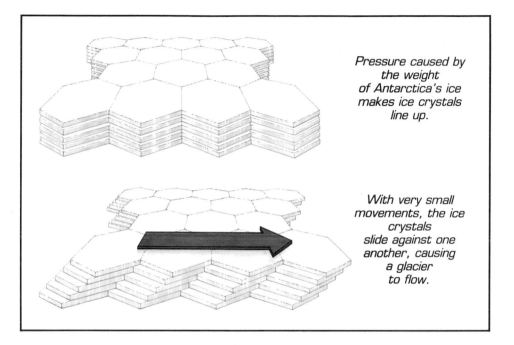

Pressure caused by the weight of Antarctica's ice makes ice crystals line up.

With very small movements, the ice crystals slide against one another, causing a glacier to flow.

very large island in the east and a string of small islands in the west. Antarctica's cold, thick, hard covering—called an **ice sheet**—began to form at least 25 million years ago.

The East Antarctic and West Antarctic ice sheets bind the continent together. From 1 to 3 miles (1.6 to 4.8 kilometers) thick, they act much like sheets do on a bed. They slide, fold, and wrinkle in the

cold climate of the southern part of our planet.

The top layer of ice, which receives the most recent snowfalls, places weight on the older layers below. The farther down from the surface, the greater the weight. Under tremendous pressure, the old ice becomes a **glacier,** a slow-moving mass of ice.

Antarctica's glaciers are steadily creeping away from the center of the continent at

different speeds. Some glaciers move only a few feet annually. The fastest ones clip along at 1.2 miles (2 kilometers) a year.

The glaciers slip into the bays that surround Antarctica and form **ice shelves** (huge coverings) over the water. The Ross Ice Shelf—the largest in Antarctica—is about the size of the state of Colorado and flows into the Ross Sea. The Ronne Ice Shelf, which lies in a curve of the Antarctic Peninsula, blends with the Weddell Sea.

Where glaciers meet the ocean, huge chunks of ice break off to form **icebergs.** The birth of an iceberg is called a **calving.** The biggest iceberg ever recorded was sighted in 1956. It calved from the Ross Ice Shelf and measured 208 miles (335 kilometers) by 60 miles (97 kilometers). This area is six times bigger than the state of Delaware!

In one of Antarctica's dry valleys, a glacier's path has gradually carved a deep swirl.

Glaciers from the East Antarctic Ice Sheet flow into the Ross Sea, forming the Ross Ice Shelf. This shelf reaches 70 feet (21 meters) above the sea and extends for hundreds of feet below the water's surface. The sea and the shelf were named after James Clark Ross, a British Antarctic explorer of the 1840s.

Hundreds of large and small icebergs calve, or break off, from the ice shelves around Antarctica. Only about one-tenth of an iceberg is visible above water.

WEIRD AND WONDERFUL

Antarctica is a land of contrasts and extremes. To humankind, it has always seemed like one of the strangest places on earth. Let's consider some of Antarctica's weird and wonderful traits.

Antarctica is the world's coldest continent. The average temperature in winter plunges to –58° F. (–50° C). A warm day in summer does not often get above 5° F (–15° C). Scientists noted one of the lowest temperatures ever recorded on our planet on July 21, 1983, at the Soviet base called Vostok. It lies in the middle of East Antarctica. The temperature that day fell to –128.6° F (–89.2° C).

The planet's windiest continent, Antarctica experiences harsh **katabatic winds** that roll down from East Antarctica's high plateau. As they approach the coast, these winds often reach speeds of about 200 miles (322 kilometers) per hour.

As the katabatic winds rush out to sea, they collide with the warmer air over the ocean. The results are violent storms that create the roughest seas in the world.

Bundled up against the cold, these children from Argentina explore the area around their country's research station on the Antarctic Peninsula.

Sailors long ago marked the locations of these rough seas on navigational charts, naming the dangerous places the Roaring Forties and the Furious Fifties. The numbers refer to latitudes on maps.

The rough seas of the Southern Ocean became the scene of The Rime of the Ancient Mariner, *a long poem of adventure and myth by the British writer Samuel Taylor Coleridge.*

Antarctica holds 70 percent of the world's entire supply of fresh (non-salty) water in ice and snow. Yet the continent receives less than 2 inches (5 centimeters) of **precipitation** (water in the form of rain and snow) a year. In comparison, Africa's Sahara Desert averages about 8 inches (20 centimeters) annually.

The interior of Antarctica is especially dry. The South Pole probably gets less than 1 inch (2.5 centimeters) of rain every year. Although Antarctica is a desert, if its ice were to melt, the oceans of the world would rise 180 feet (55 meters). This is the height of six telephone poles!

Antarctica has an average elevation above sea level of 2.5 miles (4 kilometers), making it the world's highest continent. The cold, harsh climate has contributed to Antarctica's height.

In warm areas of our planet, the heat of the sun changes surface water from a solid (ice) to a liquid (water) and then to a gas (vapor)—a process called **evaporation.** But Antarctica seldom gets warm enough for evaporation to take place. As a result, the ice on the surface builds up over time, creating thick ice sheets.

High peaks tower above the ice plateaus of East and West Antarctica. Geographers

In the summer, which lasts from December to February, the rocky, ice-free valleys of the Antarctic interior indicate where glaciers once covered the land.

The tops of the Transantarctic Mountains (right) cut between the East and West Antarctic ice sheets. A scientist (below) gazes at the snow-covered peak of Vinson Massif, which is part of the Ellsworth range that lies in West Antarctica.

(people who study the layout of the earth) think the Transantarctic Mountains were once part of the Andes, a mountain chain that stretches along western South America. Vinson Massif, the highest mountain in Antarctica, reaches 16,860 feet (5,139 meters) in elevation.

CHAPTER TWO

A DESERT AND AN OASIS

Although Antarctica itself has almost no life, the surrounding ocean teems with plants, fish, whales, seabirds, and seals. Let's look at the contrasts in the Antarctic region.

A BARREN LAND

Plants need soil and water to live, and Antarctica has little of either. Only two **species** (kinds) of flowering plants grow on the continent, compared to the thousands that thrive on nearby southern South America. Both of Antarctica's flowering species

(Left) Antarctica only has two flowering species of plants—a grass called Deschampsia antarctica *and a pink named* Colobanthus quitensis. *Life in the oceans is plentiful, however, and includes these two elephant seals (right) that communicate by making loud noises.*

survive in the mild coastal areas of the Antarctic Peninsula. Other kinds of plants are tiny **algae, mosses,** and **lichens** that develop into velvety splashes of color in the spring months.

Plants must have soil in which to grow. But in Antarctica it is almost impossible for soil to form. Katabatic winds blow away the small particles of worn rock that, without the wind, could build up into **topsoil.** Once soil has formed, the roots of plants help to hold it in place. But, with so few plants in Antarctica, the thin topsoil very easily blows away.

Along with soil, plants need water to live. Large parts of Antarctica receive almost no precipitation. In some places, rain may fall for only a few days or hours each year. The coastal regions and the Antarctic Peninsula receive more precipitation. In these places, most of the continent's algae, lichens, and mosses are found.

Plants play a large role in the **food web**—the complex chain of plants and animals that depend on one another for nourishment. A place that does not have

plants will also lack large animals that need plants or smaller plant-eating animals for food. It is not surprising, therefore, that insects are the largest animals living full-time on Antarctica. Many other animals stay on the continent part-time, moving to warmer areas in the winter.

Colorful lichens cling to the rocks of coastal Antarctica.

Magnified many times, these tiny phytoplankton are at the bottom of the Antarctic food web, providing nourishment to krill and other sea life.

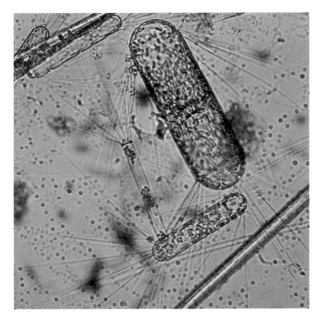

WATERS OF PLENTY

The Southern Ocean is as rich in plants and animals as the continent is barren. Some sea creatures may not spend the entire year in these waters, but the Southern Ocean still supports one of the most complicated food webs on earth. How can this chilly, churning sea be so full of life?

The answer is found in the **nutrients** and in the two gases—**carbon dioxide (CO_2)** and oxygen—that support all life. Plants need CO_2, water, nutrients and sunlight for **photosynthesis,** a food-making process. Animals eat the plants and then breathe oxygen to make energy from the food they consume. The cold waters off Antarctica contain a rich supply of nutrients and other elements necessary for photosynthesis.

In this very healthy environment, tiny plants and animals known as **plankton** thrive. Plants of this group, called **phytoplankton,** are common in the Antarctic region. The animals of plankton in the Southern Ocean, termed **zooplankton,** eat phytoplankton and sometimes one another.

An individual plankton is often too small for humans to see with the naked eye. But huge masses of plankton create brown, green, and red patches on the surface of the water. Plankton in the Southern Ocean are usually abundant and form the foundation of the Antarctic food web.

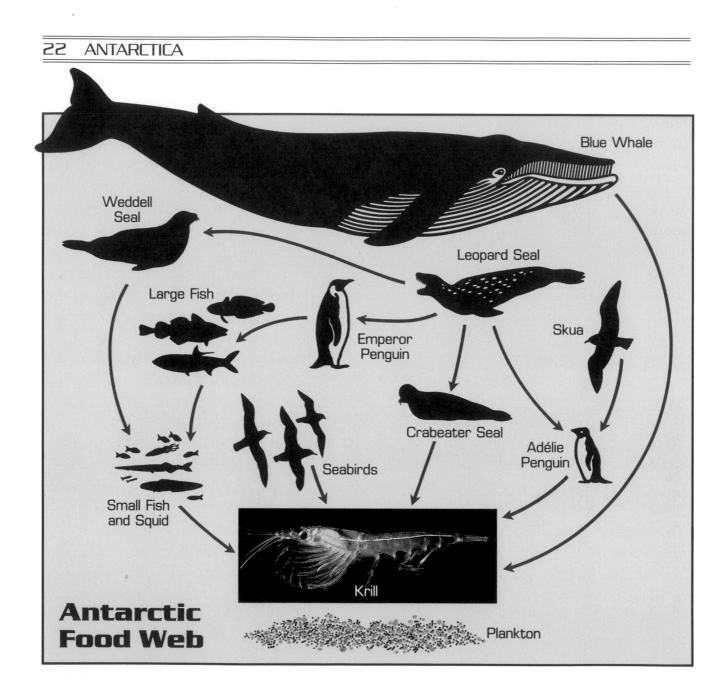

Blue Whale

Weddell Seal

Leopard Seal

Large Fish

Emperor Penguin

Skua

Crabeater Seal

Adélie Penguin

Seabirds

Small Fish and Squid

Krill

Antarctic Food Web

Plankton

They feed a vast variety of fish, birds, and animals that are much, much bigger than a single plankton.

The **Antarctic Convergence,** an ocean zone that encircles Antarctica, is known for the large number of its seabirds, including albatrosses, petrels, fulmars, shearwaters, and prions. They come to feed on the huge masses of plankton that thrive in the Southern Ocean. At the convergence, warm bottom water from northern oceans bumps into colder bottom water from the Southern Ocean. This meeting brings nutrients to the surface and produces large amounts of phytoplankton on which hungry seabirds feast.

A WHALE OF A STORY

In addition to small plants and animals, the Southern Ocean contains very large animals, including whales. Whales are

While feeding on krill, a blue whale exhales through its blowhole (the nostril in the top of its head).

Among the six species of seals in the Southern Ocean is the Weddell seal. It is named after James Weddell, a British navigator and seal hunter who traveled to the Antarctic region in the 1820s. These seals, which can remain under water for more than an hour, dive hundreds of feet in search of fish.

mammals like us. They need air to breathe and are warm-blooded. And, like human babies, young whales are fed with milk produced by their mothers.

Two kinds of whales live in the Antarctic region. Members of one group have bristly rows of plates, made of a substance called **baleen,** in the roof of the mouth. The baleen plates allow a whale to strain **krill** (tiny shrimplike zooplankton) out of seawater.

The Antarctic blue whale—the largest creature living on our planet—is a baleen whale. Other large baleen feeders in Antarctica are the fin whale, the sei whale, and the humpback whale.

The whaling industry has seriously decreased the populations of all of these species. For example, in 1930 whalers killed 30,000 blue whales in Antarctic waters alone. Out of a population that once numbered 200,000, only about 10,000 blue whales now survive.

The other kind of whale has teeth instead of baleen. These whales eat fish and squid. The sperm whale is the largest of the toothed whales. It can reach a length of 49 feet (15 meters) and can weigh 43 tons (39 metric tons). Dolphins and porpoises are related to toothed whales.

SEALS AND PENGUINS

Unlike whales, seals spend part of their time on land or on **pack ice** (large compact pieces of sea ice). With its four flippers, a seal can swim gracefully in water or can waddle on ice, snow, and rocks. Six species of seals live in Antarctica, and the largest is the elephant seal, which has a long nose. Some male elephant seals measure 23 feet (7 meters) in length and weigh up to 4 tons (3.6 metric tons).

Other seals include the leopard seal, which is known for the spots on its coat. It lives on pack ice around Antarctica and feeds on penguins. Another type, the Weddell seal, looks fat and sluggish on land, but it can dive swiftly through holes in the ice to catch fish.

Like baleen whales, crabeater seals feed on krill. These seals also live on pack ice, as do rare Ross's seals, which eat fish and squid rather than krill. Hunters in the

King penguins (right) inhabit the Antarctic Peninsula as well as some of the islands that surround the continent. Although they look like smaller versions of the larger emperor species, king penguins have different breeding locations and parenting patterns.

A lone macaroni penguin climbs the rocks on Elephant Island. This medium-sized penguin has distinctive orange feathers over its eyes. Macaronis mainly eat shrimp and other shellfish that swim near the Antarctic islands and peninsula.

1800s killed almost all fur seals, which were prized for their lush coats. Internationally protected since 1972, fur seals have slowly increased in number in recent decades.

Penguins are perhaps the most famous Antarctic wildlife. These flightless birds are well adapted for life in the cold Southern Ocean, where they spend about half their time. They use their winglike flippers to dive and swim through the water.

Found only in the Southern Hemisphere, penguins gather in huge breeding groups, or colonies, that can contain a million birds. Six species—the king, the Adélie, the chinstrap, the gentoo, the macaroni, and the rock hopper—breed on the islands that surround Antarctica and sometimes on the continent's coasts. One other type—the emperor penguin—tends to live and breed on the ice shelves.

PENGUIN PARENTS

Seven different kinds of penguins live in Antarctica. Emperor penguins are the largest in size. Some emperor penguins reach nearly 4 feet [1.2 meters] in height and weigh more than 60 pounds [27 kilograms]. They can dive deeply in Antarctic waters in search of fish and squid and also can fast [go without food] for months.

Male emperor penguins huddle together as they incubate unhatched eggs.

In March, the birds move inland from the coastal ice shelves to claim their breeding ground and to find a mate. While fasting, each female emperor penguin lays an egg in May or June. Needing to resupply her body with food, she then leaves her mate in charge of the unhatched egg and treks back to the ocean.

For two months, the male emperor penguin **incubates** the egg, keeping it warm and protected so it will hatch. First he places the egg on top of his feather-covered feet. Then he wraps the egg in a flap of skin that hangs from his stomach. Incubating males huddle closely together against the cold, the wind, and the darkness. They do not eat but instead live on their reserves of blubber [fat]. These father penguins often lose half of their body weight during the incubation period.

After feeding for several weeks, the female returns in July or August, when her egg is ready to hatch. To nourish her new baby, a mother penguin throws up food she has stored in her body and then feeds it to her chick. The male, who has fasted for about four months, waddles off in search of a bellyful of fish and squid. Parents later take turns watching over the growing chick until it can dive and swim in search of its own food.

CHAPTER THREE

"NO ONE COMES HERE CASUALLY"

In many parts of the world, explorers have made important discoveries by accident. This seldom happens in Antarctica. On our planet's harsh and barren southern continent, explorers have died because they did not prepare carefully. As one scientific visitor said, "No one comes here casually."

Ui-te-Rangiora, who came from an island in the South Pacific Ocean, is considered the first Antarctic explorer. He saw the frozen Southern Ocean in about A.D. 650. Centuries later, in 1738, the cold, fog-covered place was noticed by a French sailing captain who brought back the first clear accounts of this strange land.

FINDING THE CONTINENT

In the late 1700s, several nations sent expeditions to the Southern Ocean. The main

(Left) *During the mildest summer months, the ships that travel to Antarctica usually meet only scattered blocks of ice.* (Above) *In the 1770s, Captain James Cook of Britain explored the seas very near the continent without ever seeing it.*

purpose of these trips was to observe a rare movement of the planet Venus. But Great Britain also asked one of its explorers, Captain James Cook, to try to find a legendary southern continent before French explorers did.

Cook led several expeditions to the southern seas between 1770 and 1775. He sailed very close to the coast of Antarctica but never saw it. His reports described vast numbers of seals and whales. As a result, commercial hunters of seals and whales were soon finding rich harvests in the Southern Ocean.

During the early 1800s, sailors, explorers, and sealers from various nations made sightings of land in the Southern Ocean. Some visitors may have landed on parts of the ice shelf. These people each found a piece of the continental puzzle.

The U.S. naval explorer Charles Wilkes gets the credit for proving that Antarctica was a real continent and not just a big piece of ice. Between 1838 and 1842, Wilkes led the U.S. Exploring Expedition, which made numerous consistent sightings and measurements of East Antarctica. Wilkes, however, never landed on the continent.

Cook's descriptions of large numbers of seals and whales attracted hunters of these animals to the Antarctic region. At first, whalers had little success in catching their prey. In fact, the flick of a whale's powerful tail could capsize or even destroy a small whaling boat.

Charles Wilkes led a four-year U.S. expedition to Antarctica in the mid-1800s. Measurements of the coasts made by Wilkes and his crew prompted him to declare the ice mass in the Southern Ocean to be a continent. Wilkes Land was named in his honor.

THE RACE TO THE POLE

In the early twentieth century, several nations realized that Antarctica was the last unexplored continent on earth. They be-lieved that fame and glory would come to the country that endured hardships to learn about this mysterious place.

In June 1910, Robert Falcon Scott of Great Britain set sail for Antarctica in the *Terra Nova*. He and his team wanted to be the first explorers to reach the South Pole. Meanwhile, a ship named the *Fram* left Norway for the same destination. The captain of the Norwegian vessel was Roald Amundsen. These two explorers were rivals racing toward the South Pole.

Amundsen's Route

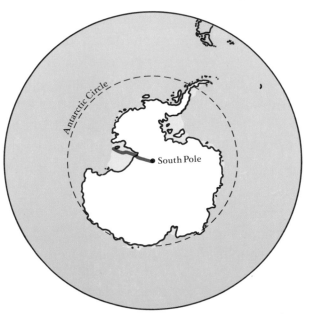

This painting shows Amundsen and his three companions at the South Pole on December 14, 1911. They are standing at attention in front of the Norwegian flag.

On October 19, 1911, Amundsen left his ship in the Bay of Whales in the Ross Sea to find the South Pole. The Norwegian group of four men benefited from warm polar clothing, and they traveled on skis. The expedition's 52 dogs pulled sleds loaded with food and other supplies. Amundsen's team reached the South Pole on December 14, 1911, planting the flag of Norway on the spot. After two days of exploring the area, the group returned to camp.

Unlike his rival, Scott thought skis and dogsleds were not useful in polar exploration. Instead, he brought sleds with motors

to Antarctica. In addition, his men pulled their own gear, a very slow, exhausting way to travel.

Scott and his group left their camp on the Ross Ice Shelf on November 1, 1911. The party was made up of 16 men, the motorized sleds, some ponies, and a few dogs. The sleds soon broke down. Clumsy on the snow and ice, the ponies had to be shot. Finally, Scott sent the dogs and all but four men back to base camp.

The five men continued toward the South Pole, even though they did not have enough food. The small group reached the South Pole on January 17, 1912, but the Norwegian flag told them they had been beaten to their goal.

Cold, tired, and disappointed, Scott's party began the trek back to base camp.

Scott's Route

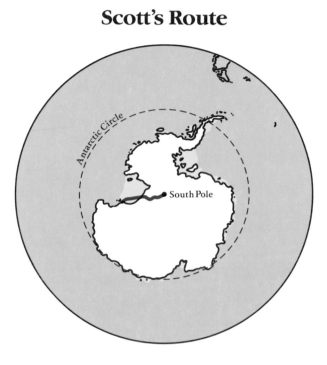

Antarctic Circle

South Pole

Robert Scott's weary team peers into the camera on January 17, 1912, when the five British men reached the South Pole after the Norwegians did. The photo was taken by Henry Bowers (seated left) who pulled a string attached to the camera shutter. The negative of the photo was found with the frozen bodies of Bowers, Scott (standing center), and Edward Wilson (seated right). After leaving the pole, Lawrence Oates (standing left) was injured and sacrificed himself in an effort to save his colleagues. Edgar Evans (standing right) died of exposure soon after this picture was taken.

Pulling the sleds made the men very weak. One member, Edgar Evans, suffered badly from **frostbite** and soon died. Another, Lawrence Oates, left his tent one night and was never seen again. The last three men—Scott, Edward Wilson, and Henry Bowers —were caught in a blizzard for nine days. They froze to death in their tents. Eight months later, a search party found them in their icy graves.

ERNEST SHACKLETON
An Enduring Explorer

The British explorer Ernest Shackleton led two Antarctic expeditions. The first one, in 1909, came within 97 miles [156 kilometers] of the South Pole before the explorer's team ran out of food and had to return to base camp. His second trip, from 1914 to 1916, was a failure in some ways, because he and his group never even landed on the continent. Yet, Shackleton brought home every member of both expeditions because he put the welfare of his crew above his personal Antarctic goals.

In August 1914, Shackleton and 28 men sailed from England on the *Endurance*. The expedition's aim was to cross Antarctica from the Weddell Sea to the Ross Sea. When the crew reached the Southern Ocean, unusually thick ice slowed their progress. By January 1915, pack ice had trapped the ship. Hoping the ice would break up, the crew waited for nine months before abandoning the *Endurance*. In October, they moved their supplies and three small boats onto a nearby **ice floe** and watched as ice crushed the ship.

At this point, the crew was far from land in rough seas and had limited food. Shackleton carefully rationed (restricted) food supplies and organized the crew to haul the boats across the ice. Fierce blizzards, frostbite, and food shortages made life miserable. After four months, the group reached Elephant Island, an uninhabited island about 550 miles [885 kilometers] southeast of South America.

Ernest Shackleton stands with one of his sled dogs during his 1909 expedition to the South Pole.

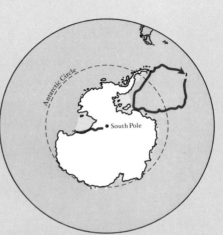

[Left] *From Elephant Island, the excited crew of the* Endurance *waves to Shackleton and a rescue boat in 1916.*

Although now on land, Shackleton knew that the nearest settlement lay 800 miles [1,287 kilometers] away on South Georgia, an island whalers used as a base. In April 1916, Shackleton and five men set out in one of the battered boats. Cold and tired, the group reached the southern coast of South Georgia in 18 days. But the whaling station was across low mountains on the northern coast. After a rest, Shackleton and two colleagues crossed the mountains, arriving at the station on May 20, 1916.

Pack ice twice prevented Shackleton from leaving South Georgia for Elephant Island. In August 1916, Shackleton succeeded in his third attempt and returned to rescue his crew. He found them weak but still alive.

A scientist who knew Robert Scott, Roald Amundsen, and Shackleton once wrote: "As a scientific leader give me Scott; for swift and efficient polar travel, Amundsen; but when things are hopeless and there seems no way out, get down on your knees and pray for Shackleton."

THE MODERN ERA

A U.S. naval pilot named Richard Byrd was the first person to fly over the South Pole. Byrd's trip in 1929 revealed parts of Antarctica that no one had ever seen. Byrd established Little America, a research station, on the Ross Ice Shelf. The station's main purpose was to collect scientific data, but Little America also proved that humans could survive in the harshest environment on earth.

Airplanes and other modern equipment changed the nature of polar exploration. In the early 1950s, scientists decided to dedicate a special time—the International Geophysical Year (IGY)—to the study of three deep mysteries, namely outer space, the ocean floor, and Antarctica. The year of study actually took 18 months—from July 1, 1957, to December 31, 1958.

The IGY was a great success and became an excellent example of cooperation among nations. During the IGY, 12 countries established research stations on Antarctica and the surrounding islands. These nations included the United States, the Soviet Union, Japan, Britain, Argentina, Belgium, and Norway.

McMurdo Station, the large U.S. research base on the Ross Ice Shelf, displays a statue of Richard Byrd, the first person to fly over the South Pole. Behind the monument are the flags of countries with research bases on the continent.

Entire families live at Argentina's Esperanza Station, which was set up after the International Geophysical Year of the late 1950s.

SIX ACROSS THE ICE

Until the 1980s, no one had crossed Antarctica without using machines. That changed on July 27, 1989, when six people from six countries set out on three dogsleds. They had about 40 dogs with them. The trek was called the International Trans-Antarctica Expedition.

The leaders were Will Steger of the United States and Jean-Louis Etienne of France. The other members of the team came from Japan, Britain, the Soviet Union, and China. Choosing the longest route across the continent, the six men covered 3,741 miles (6,020 kilometers). This is the same as the distance between New York, New York, and Barcelona, Spain.

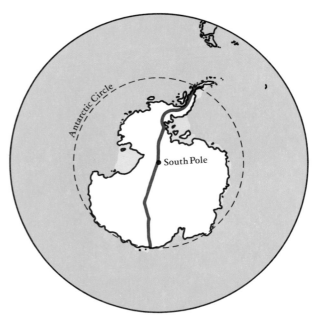

(Right) The route of the International Trans-Antarctica Expedition.

Even with modern polar gear, it was a difficult journey. **Whiteouts,** a weather condition that happens when harsh winds fill the air with snow, often forced the party to stop because the trekkers could not see where they were going. Snowstorms also buried 3 of 12 places where the explorers had stored food. Some of the dogs got so tired they had to be removed by airplane.

Despite these obstacles, the International Trans-Antarctica Expedition arrived at its destination on March 3, 1990. The trek's members showed that six people from very different cultures could work toward a common goal under the world's worst traveling conditions. As Steger put it, "We proved in the end that we weren't very different after all."

Holding the flags of their nations, the members of the expedition pose with a few of the sled dogs. The explorers are (left to right) **Keizo Funatsu of Japan, Geoff Somers of Britain, Qin Dahe of China, Will Steger of the United States, Jean-Louis Etienne of France, and Victor Boyarsky of the Soviet Union.**

SLED DOGS
Loyal from "Hup" to "Whoa"

Polar sled drivers have written many stories praising their loyal, sturdy sled dogs. A sled dog is not a certain breed but simply a dog that pulls a sled. The best long-distance sled dogs are strong, alert, and eager to run. In addition, the dogs are responsive to the sled driver's commands, which include "hup" [go] and "whoa" [stop].

A thick coat, toes that are close together, and tough pads on the feet help sled dogs thrive in cold polar conditions. Owners breed dogs with these traits to get a sled dog of stamina and spirit. Some of the best sled dogs are huskies that come from regions near the North Pole, such as Siberia, Alaska, and Greenland.

Sled dogs usually pull in teams. The strongest dogs are harnessed nearest the sled. The others—who are either good pullers or skilled at making turns—are lined up along the harness in pairs. At the front is the lead dog, who has the respect of the other dogs and of the driver. This dog easily follows commands, has good control of the other dogs, and boldly handles dangerous situations. Together, driver and dogs brave the fierce winds, blowing snow, and other hazards of polar travel.

Blowing snow sometimes made travel difficult for the sled dogs and drivers of the International Trans-Antarctica Expedition.

CHAPTER FOUR

A WILDERNESS AT RISK

Antarctica is the most unspoiled place on earth. But the continent and the oceans around it have withstood many threats. In recent years, more people have begun to take care of our planet's natural environment. We can preserve Antarctica—and the earth—by learning from our mistakes.

A KILLING SPREE

Captain Cook returned from one of his voyages in the 1770s with reports of huge colonies of fur seals on Antarctic islands.

(Left) Penguins cling to a crystal blue iceberg. The deep color of the ice indicates its extreme age. Over time, as layers of ice are packed down, air trapped within the ice is squeezed out. Airless ice is very dense and takes on the unusual blue tint.

Sealers swarmed to the Southern Ocean, and their hunting methods nearly eliminated every fur seal in Antarctica.

Whaling began in the Antarctic region in the mid-1800s. But, in the rough Southern Ocean, the whales were hard to catch. Within a few decades, steam-powered ships and explosive harpoons changed the balance. The new ships could ram through ice and travel fast. The new harpoons could be fired from the bow of a boat a long way from an escaping whale. Whalers now had the advantage over their prey, and by 1904 Antarctic whaling was in full swing.

At first, the hunters took only **whalebone** (the baleen) and **blubber,** the animal's layer of fat that is rich in oil. From the whalebone, manufacturers produced combs, fans, and inserts in women's dresses. Other industries refined the blubber into

41

a fuel oil for lamps. The rest of the dead whale was left to rot in the ocean.

In the 1920s, people learned how to make margarine from whale oil. Designers invented factory ships, which could process entire whales while at sea. Some peo-

In the 1800s and early 1900s, it was fashionable in Europe and in the United States for a woman to have a tiny waist. Manufacturers of women's underclothes sewed strips of whalebone—the tough, flexible baleen from a whale's mouth—into corsets (tight-fitting undergarments) to achieve the desired curve and width.

ple began to value whale meat as a source of food.

As a result of these changes, the large-scale slaughter of whales began. At a peak in the 1930–1931 season, whalers killed more than 40,000 whales. By the late 1930s, the large whales—the blue and fin whales especially—were disappearing. But whalers continued to hunt them.

In 1946, the major whaling nations formed the International Whaling Commission (IWC). Its goal was to protect whales from being overhunted so that the whaling industry could survive.

Although the IWC set quotas (limits) for the number of whales that could be killed each year, the quotas were high, and whale populations continued to decline. Conservationists (people who work to protect the earth's environment) have pointed out that more whales were killed after the IWC was organized than before its existence. In 1962, for example, whalers killed about 67,000 whales.

In the 1970s, conservationists began to fear that whales might become **extinct** (cease to exist). They worked harder to stop the slaughter and to preserve the remaining whales. After a decade of effort, they had made significant progress.

The IWC continually lowered the quotas, so that fewer whales could be killed legally. In 1982, the IWC voted to halt the killing of whales altogether for 10 years beginning in 1985. Japan, Iceland, and Norway, however, continue to kill whales in the name of scientific research, and the Japanese still eat whale meat as food.

FOOD FOR THOUGHT

Kril—an old Norwegian word meaning "young creepy-crawly fish,"—is a good description of the little shrimplike zooplankton that whales and other sea life eat. A Soviet fishing boat first harvested krill from Antarctic waters in 1964. The animals—which are high in protein and rich in vitamin A—feed people, cattle, chickens, and farm-raised fish.

Other countries—including Japan, Poland, South Korea, and Taiwan—followed

Japan is one of the few nations of the world that is still hunting whales. Here, a Japanese boat drags a whale's carcass before bringing it on board.

the Soviet Union's lead. Most of these nations stopped fishing for krill in the 1970s and early 1980s, when the work cost too much money. In the late 1980s, however, the Japanese invented a way to process krill on board their ships. The Soviets and the Japanese have become the world's largest harvesters of krill in Antarctica.

Conservationists who look back on the collapse of Antarctica's populations of seals and whales worry that someday humans will take too many krill. Krill are the most important link in the Antarctic food web, nourishing fish, seals, seabirds, penguins, and whales. If the krill population declines, these animal species could starve.

Krill are in danger from another people-made problem—the ozone hole. **Ozone** is a gas that, in the upper atmosphere, shields our planet from the sun's **ultraviolet (UV) light.** Too much of this light can hurt plants and animals.

Scientists discovered that chemicals in the air called **chloro-fluoro-carbons (CFCs)** were drifting upward into the layer of ozone. At this height, the CFCs break apart, and parts of the chemicals destroy the ozone. In 1983, scientists noticed that the ozone layer was thinning over Antarctica. The weakening shield lets more UV light reach the earth. High levels of UV light may already be slowing the growth of the phytoplankton on which Antarctic krill feed.

Huge swarms of krill (below) are the food source for most of the animals that live in Antarctica. Endangering this food supply is the earth's thinning layer of ozone, a gas that shields the krill from harmful sunlight. The purple splotch over Antarctica on this computer image (right) shows where the ozone layer is dangerously thin.

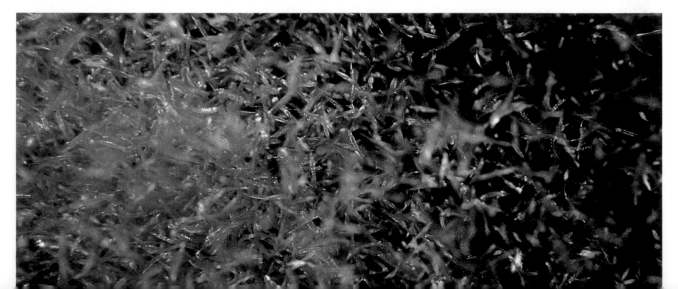

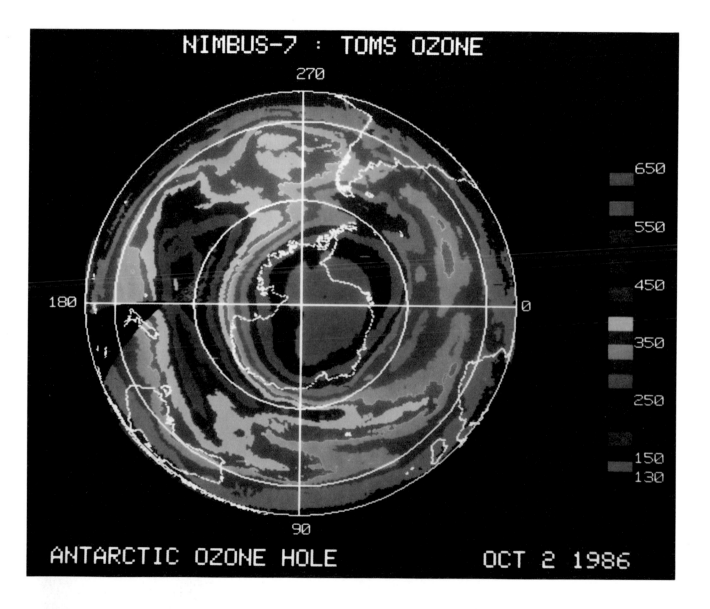

Rich countries produce and use lots of CFCs. The chemicals are the coolants in refrigerators and air conditioners. CFCs also appear in many cleaning fluids and are needed to make some kinds of plastics.

Many nations have agreed to stop making CFCs by the year 2000. Even with a world-wide ban, it would take more than 100 years for the CFCs already swirling around our planet to disappear. As a result, the ozone hole will not go away soon and will probably get larger.

GOING UP IN SMOKE

We humans burn **fossil fuels**—petroleum and coal—in our cars, factories, and furnaces. The burning of these fuels pumps large amounts of CO_2 into the earth's atmosphere. As CO_2 rises, it traps the sun's heat, preventing it from returning to the atmosphere. This action, which imitates the way glass traps heat in a greenhouse, is often called the **greenhouse effect.** Scientists think that the increase in CO_2 may magnify the greenhouse ef-

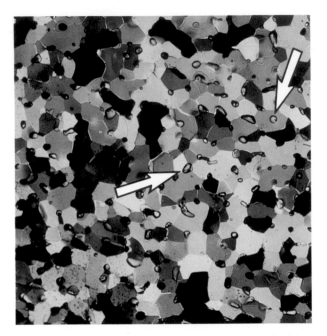

Arrows point to gas-filled air bubbles trapped between magnified Antarctic ice crystals. Scientists drilled 180 feet (55 meters) to obtain this core sample.

fect, causing the earth's temperature to rise over the next several decades. Scientists name this people-made problem **global warming.**

Making studies of global warming and of the greenhouse effect are among the main jobs of scientists in Antarctica. They drill deeply into Antarctica's ice to take **core samples.** Scientists examine the chemicals and gases trapped in this ancient ice. Studies of core samples suggest that we now have more CO_2 in our atmosphere than ever before.

Eager to take photos of Antarctica's unusual wildlife, tourists can frighten or bother seals, penguins, and other animals.

What effect would global warming have on Antarctica? The Antarctic ice sheets could melt, causing the ocean to rise and flood coastal cities. The fresh water from the ice sheets would mix with the ocean's salt water, changing the salt content of the ocean. This shift could hurt all the plants and animals that live in the ocean.

CLEANING UP OUR ACT

About 3,000 tourists traveled annually to Antarctica by ship in the early 1990s, and every year more people want to visit. Vacationers often hurt wildlife by making too much noise or by getting too close to breeding colonies. These actions sometimes stop the animals from mating and having babies. Some tourists leave litter and disturb scientific projects.

In 1989, an Argentine supply ship carrying people to the Antarctic Peninsula sank offshore. The vacationers escaped, but 170,000 gallons (643,518 liters) of petroleum spilled. Hundreds of birds died, and scientific studies were destroyed.

A COLD LABORATORY

It's hard to imagine living and working in the extremely low temperatures and harsh winds of Antarctica, but several thousand scientists do just that every year. Wearing layers of protective clothing, researchers in many fields get on with their work.

To piece together Antarctica's history as a continent, **geologists** examine rocks to find out how ice may have shaped and moved them. Because the types of rocks found on Antarctica are also found on South America, Australia, and Africa, geologists believe that Antarctica was once connected to these other continents.

Glaciologists study ice by drilling deeply for core samples. The depth of each layer of ice in the samples can be measured. From the annual buildup of ice, a glaciologist can tell how cold the weather was in Antarc-

A geologist uses a Geiger counter to test Antarctica's rocks for radioactivity.

tica in a given year. From air bubbles trapped in the ancient ice, these scientists can also identify gases, such as carbon dioxide, that were once in the air.

Special clothing is needed by **marine biologists,** who dive into the chilly Southern Ocean wearing extra-thick wet suits. These scientists study the creatures that live under water. Above ground, other **biologists** find out about the animals that breed in Antarctica's cold climate.

Paleontologists spend their time examining fossils—the preserved remains of living things that once inhabited Antarctica. These scientists have discovered that the continent wasn't always as cold and barren as it is now. In fact, millions of years ago, the place was full of tree ferns, reptiles, and dinosaurs!

Scientists have not set a good example either. About 4,000 people work at the 40 research stations in Antarctica. Every year, more scientists want to go there to study.

Research stations have dumped their raw sewage into the ocean, have burned trash in open pits, and have discarded machinery on the exposed land. In 1989, 52,000 gallons (196,841 liters) of petroleum leaked from a storage tank at McMurdo Station, a large U.S. research base, onto the Ross Ice Shelf. At Dumont d'Urville, the French research station, workers destroyed part of a penguin colony to build a landing strip for airplanes.

In 1987, the environmental group Greenpeace set up a station in Antarctica to monitor the other bases. Various governments have arranged cleanups as a result of inspections by Greenpeace. In 1990, for example, the United States added $10 million to its Antarctic research budget to protect the environment and has since cleaned up McMurdo Station.

The United States came under pressure in the late 1980s and early 1990s to clean up McMurdo Station (left). Although much remains to be done, U.S. efforts have improved conditions on some parts of the base (right).

CHAPTER FIVE

PROTECTING ANTARCTICA

Since the International Geophysical Year in the late 1950s, nations have worked peacefully side by side to learn about Antarctica. If this cooperative effort is to continue, all of us need to speak our minds about our southernmost continent.

COMMON INTERESTS

After Antarctica was discovered, people from various countries came to the Southern Ocean to make money from hunting seals and whales. In later years, nations felt that Antarctica had additional sources of wealth, possibly precious fuels and

(Left) With this illustration, Catalina Guzman of Los Angeles, California, expresses her opinion about Antarctica's future. (Right) An exposed rock shows Antarctica's copper deposits.

minerals. To secure the rights to the valuable goods, countries tried to establish authority over Antarctica by saying that parts of the continent belonged to them. These nations included France, Britain, Chile, Argentina, and Norway.

To complicate matters, Britain, Argentina, and Chile all claimed authority over the same territory—the Antarctic Peninsula. People worried that these overlapping claims would lead to war. In addition, the long-standing rivals for world power—the Soviet Union and the United States—were very interested in Antarctica, even though neither nation claimed ownership.

THE ANTARCTIC TREATY

International tensions endangered the future of Antarctica until the IGY, when scientists from around the world spent 18 months studying the continent. These scholars peacefully shared information, and their harmony created goodwill among nations. This cooperation led to the negotiation of a treaty to protect Antarctica.

In 1961, the representatives of 12 nations signed the Antarctic Treaty, which dealt with issues regarding the future of Antarctica. Since then, many other countries have agreed to follow the treaty's goals.

As long as it is in force, the treaty guarantees these four things:

Antarctica will remain open for scientific research to nations who agree to the treaty.

No military bases can be built on Antarctica.

No testing of nuclear weapons or dumping of nuclear waste is allowed on Antarctica.

No claims of ownership are recognized or denied, and no new claims of ownership can be made.

The Antarctic Treaty sets Antarctica aside as a place for the peaceful pursuit of science. The nations that signed the treaty decided to wait 30 years—until 1991—to see how the treaty worked. In April 1991, these countries met in Madrid, Spain, to review the results of three decades of cooperation.

Triangles mark international claims to Antarctic territory. The Antarctic Treaty, signed in 1961 and reviewed in 1991, makes no effort to recognize or to deny these ownership claims. In this way, treaty signers have avoided conflict, but they have also avoided some of the responsibility for protecting the continent.

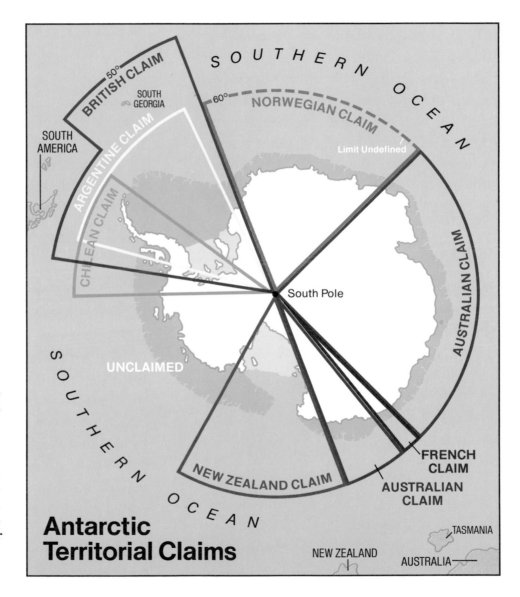

Antarctic Territorial Claims

One of the most delicate issues talked about in Spain concerned Antarctica's minerals. Some countries want to keep open the option of mining, while others want to make sure mining never happens on Antarctica. After much discussion, the signers agreed to a moratorium (temporary ban) on mining to last 50 years. By agreeing to this long wait, the treaty signers have given Antarctica a chance to survive unchanged for five more decades.

Writing letters to local, regional, national, and international leaders gives us a chance to influence decisions about Antarctica.

WHAT CAN WE DO?

It may not seem very easy to protect a place as distant as Antarctica is. But many of our human actions have already affected the continent, even though we live very far from it. Here are some ideas about what all of us can do to protect Antarctica and to lessen the negative impact we have on the global environment.

WRITE LETTERS. Put pressure on the governments, agencies, and people who are making the decisions that affect the future of Antarctica. These groups include the heads of your own government, the leaders of nations that still hunt whales, and the organizations that send researchers to Antarctica. Tell these people what you think should be done with Antarctica. Remind them of the human actions that have already had a harmful impact on the continent. Public libraries usually have the addresses you'll need.

JOIN AND SUPPORT ORGANIZATIONS THAT PRESERVE ANTARCTICA. Some of these groups work throughout the world to press leaders for more safeguards and to educate people about the dangers to Antarctica.

AVOID STYROFOAM AND OTHER PLASTIC FOAM CONTAINERS. Manufactured from CFCs, goods made of plastic foam also release CFCs when they are burned. CFCs have thinned the ozone layer, which is particularly fragile over Antarctica. Ask your favorite fast-food chain to wrap your hamburger in paper rather than in Styrofoam. Let the restaurant know why you are asking for a paper container.

REDUCE, REUSE, RECYCLE, DO WITHOUT. Our impact on the earth's environment is directly related to the way we buy, how much garbage we make, and how we throw away our garbage. When we buy less, we have less to dump. When we reuse or recycle, we decrease the need for fossil fuels to run factories that make new products. When we do without, we take action against the huge amounts of the earth's resources that we consume.

USE OTHER TRANSPORTATION BESIDES CARS. Exhaust from cars adds CO_2 to our atmosphere, worsening the

Riding buses, instead of using cars, helps to reduce carbon dioxide in the air.

greenhouse effect. It leads to global warming, which may have a terrible impact on Antarctica and on the world. Mass-transit systems—buses, subways, and trains—are good alternatives to cars because they carry many people at one time. And bicycles are the cleanest form of transportation.

STUDENTS SHARE AN ANTARCTIC ADVENTURE

In 1989, as the International Trans-Antarctica Expedition was about to start, Student Ocean Challenge (SOC) wondered how kids could share in this exciting trek. An independent educational group in Rhode Island, SOC supplies teaching materials to classrooms. The group focuses on issues that involve the ocean and other global environments.

During the 1989–1990 school year, with SOC's help, students throughout the United States followed the progress of the six explorers as they crossed Antarctica by dogsled. Nearly every week, the team talked by radio or satellite to its support ship in the Southern Ocean. These reports were transmitted to SOC and then to schools participating in the program.

Classroom activities taught students about the geography of the continent, about dogs and dogsleds, and about special foods and clothing needed in Antarctica's climate. The students also learned about the animals living in and around the continent and about the Antarctic Treaty that protects them. Some students drew illustrations and wrote essays about Antarctica for a nationwide contest. Other students participated in the celebrations that welcomed home the explorers.

Chris Poole of Caribou, Maine, submitted this drawing as part of the Antarctica Contest sponsored by Student Ocean Challenge.

ADDITIONAL SAFEGUARDS

Over the years, the signers of the Antarctic Treaty have agreed to additional international laws that protect natural resources on the continent and in the oceans. In 1964, several new measures were passed to conserve Antarctic plants and animals. In 1972, Antarctic seals won protection.

Ten years later, the signers approved the Convention for the Conservation of Antarctic Marine (sea-based) Living Resources. This act is designed to keep krill from being overharvested. In making these changes, the voting nations have learned from the past and are looking to the future.

In the 1980s and early 1990s, some countries, including a few that had signed the Antarctic Treaty, joined a popular movement that wants to make Antarctica our planet's first world park. Such a park would prevent any development of Antarctica that would harm the continent or its wildlife. Although this idea has not been adopted by the majority of the signers, it suggests that many people around the

Members of Greenpeace hold banners that encourage people to make Antarctica our planet's first world park.

world are concerned about the future of Antarctica.

Despite the heated discussions about mining Antarctica, the Antarctic Treaty is still one of the most promising agreements ever arranged among nations. It has protected the continent for 30 years and has taught us that cooperation is not a dream.

Within this spirit, our challenge is to find a way to preserve and learn from our planet's last wilderness. Antarctica is where the cycle of global abuse can stop.

ORGANIZATIONS

THE ANTARCTICA PROJECT
707 D Street SE
Washington, D.C. 20003

GREENPEACE
1436 U Street NW
Washington, D.C. 20009

NATIONAL AUDUBON SOCIETY
666 Pennsylvania Avenue SE
Washington, D.C. 20003

NATIONAL SCIENCE FOUNDATION
Publications Unit Room 232
Division of Administrative Services
1800 G Street NW
Washington, D.C. 20550

THE WILDERNESS SOCIETY
900 17th Street NW
Washington, D.C. 20006

**WORLD WILDLIFE FUND/
CONSERVATION FOUNDATION**
1250 24th Street NW
Washington, D.C. 20037

Photo Acknowledgments

Photographs are used courtesy of: pp. 1, 10 (right), 25, D. B. Siniff; pp. 4, 39, Rick Ridgeway APA/Blackstar; p. 6, NASA; pp. 10 (left), 12, 13 (bottom), 17 (top), 20–22, 24, 48, 49 (left and right), 60–62, National Science Foundation; pp. 13 (top), 17 (bottom), 18, 27, 36, 37 (top), 40, 59 (top and bottom), John Splettstoesser; pp. 14, 19, 51, David Chittenden; p. 15, Independent Picture Service; pp. 16, 47, Stuart Klipper; p. 23, Susan Kruse/National Marine Fisheries Service; p. 26, © G. Prance/Visuals Unlimited; p. 28, S. Stone/University of Minnesota; pp. 29, 32, 34, 42, Mansell Collection; p. 30, Kendal Whaling Museum, Sharon, Massachusetts; p. 31, United States Naval Academy Museum; p. 33 (right), UPI/Bettmann; p. 35 (left), Library of Congress; p. 38, Dayton Hudson; pp. 43, 57, © Morgan/Greenpeace; p. 44, Norbert Wu; p. 45, NASA/Goddard Space Flight Center; p. 46, Anthony J. Gow, Cold Regions Research and Engineering Laboratory, Department of the Army; p. 54, Patricia Drentea; p. 55, Metropolitan Transit Commission, Minneapolis. Charts and illustrations by: pp. 9, 11, 22, 31 (right), 33 (left); 35 (right), 37 (bottom), 53, Laura Westlund; p. 50, Catalina Guzman/Soto Street Elementary; p. 56, Chris Poole/Connor Consolidated.

Front cover: D. B. Siniff
Back Cover (left and right): David Chittenden

algae (AL-jee): small plants that often grow in water or in damp areas.

Antarctic Convergence: an irregular ocean ring that surrounds Antarctica. In this zone, the cold bottom waters from the Southern Ocean converge with (meet) warmer bottom waters from oceans to the north. This convergence brings nutrients (foods) to the surface.

baleen: the rows of thin, flexible strips in the jaw of a toothless whale that allow it to sift small animals out of seawater. Manufacturers of combs and other products called the baleen **whalebone.**

biologist: a person who studies living things.

blubber: a thick layer of fat on a whale, seal, or penguin.

calving (KAAV-ing): the separation of a piece of ice from a larger ice mass to form an iceberg.

This southern elephant seal's layer of blubber keeps it warm in the cold Southern Ocean.

Flat-topped tabular icebergs calve from ice shelves.

carbon dioxide (CO₂): a gas that is naturally found in the air. CO_2 also comes from burning wood, from running vehicles on gasoline, and from exhaling.

chloro-fluoro-carbons (CFCs): chemicals made up of chlorine, fluorine, and carbon that have many industrial uses. CFCs are used in making plastic packaging, cleaning fluids, and air coolants.

A glaciologist checks the layers in a core sample he has just taken.

core sample: a long, narrow column of material obtained by drilling deeply with a hollow tube. In Antarctica, the drill gathers samples from many different layers of ice that formed millions of years ago.

evaporation: the process that changes water from a liquid to a gas (vapor).

extinct: no longer existing.

food web: a group of plants and animals, each of which is a source of food for the next member in the web.

fossil fuels: substances, such as coal and petroleum, that slowly developed from the remains of living things.

frostbite: a very painful injury that results from exposing the body—especially the ears, nose, hands, and feet—to extreme cold.

geologist (jee-AHL-uh-jist): a person who studies rocks.

glacier (GLAY-sher): a huge mass of ice that moves slowly through mountain valleys or over land.

glaciologist: a person who studies ice.

global warming: an increase in the earth's average temperature that may be caused by the greenhouse effect.

greenhouse effect: the result of the sun's heat becoming trapped in the atmosphere by gases in the same way that glass traps heat in a greenhouse.

iceberg: a piece of ice that has completely broken off from an ice shelf or glacier and that floats in the sea. In some cases, only a small part of the iceberg can be seen above the ocean's surface.

ice floe (FLOW): a thick, flat piece of floating ice that has broken off from an ice shelf.

ice sheet: a vast, flat mass of ice and snow that covers a large land area.

ice shelf: a large, thick piece of floating ice that is attached to a coastline.

incubate (ING-kew-bayt): to warm an egg with the body so that the egg can hatch.

katabatic wind: a fierce wind caused by the rapid flow of cold air down a mountain slope.

krill: shrimplike animals that are the main source of food for baleen whales and other sea animals.

lichen (LY-kun): a complex, colorful plant made up of an alga and a fungus growing together on a solid surface.

magma: hot, melted rock.

marine biologist: a person who studies sea-based living things.

moss: a plant with small leafy stems. Mosses often grow together and cover a solid surface.

nutrient (NOO-tree-int): a substance, such as nitrogen or phosphorus, used as food by plants or animals.

ozone: a gas found in the upper atmosphere that shields the earth by absorbing the sun's harmful rays.

When they need to move fast, emperor penguins flop on their stomachs and slide across the ice shelf.

In warm weather, pack ice gradually melts and becomes part of the Southern Ocean.

pack ice: blocks of ice that form on the surface of the sea and that often are broken into pieces by wind or currents.

paleontologist (pay-lee-ahn-TAHL-uh-jist): a person who studies fossils.

photosynthesis (fote-oh-SIN-thuh-suss): the chemical process by which plants make their own food. The process uses carbon dioxide, water, nutrients, and sunlight.

phytoplankton (fight-oh-PLANK-tin): tiny plants of the plankton group that are moved in water by waves or currents.

plankton: tiny plants and animals in water that are the first links in the food web.

precipitation (pree-sip-ih-TAY-shun): Water—including rain, snow, sleet, and hail—that falls to earth from the atmosphere.

species (SPEE-sheez): a kind of living thing.

topsoil: the surface layer of dirt in which plants grow.

ultraviolet (UV) light: a ray of sunlight that humans cannot see directly. The shortest UV rays harm living things, and only some of the rays are absorbed by the earth's ozone layer.

whalebone: (see **baleen**).

whiteout: a weather condition in which loose or falling snow is blown into a dense blizzard, blocking vision and preventing movement.

zooplankton (zoh-uh-PLANK-tin): tiny animals of the plankton group that can move themselves in water.

INDEX